This book is published strictly for historical purposes.
The Naval and Military Press Ltd
expressly bears no responsibility or liability of any type,
to any first, second or third party, for any harm,
injury or loss whatsoever.

THE ART OF BOXING
AND
HINTS ON TRAINING

Frontispiece.

THE AUTHOR'S FAVOURITE POSE.

THE
ART OF BOXING
AND
HINTS ON TRAINING

BY
CHIEF STAFF-INSTRUCTOR J. O'NEIL
ROYAL NAVY
Boxing Instructor, Royal Naval School of Physical Training

The Naval & Military Press Ltd

Published by

The Naval & Military Press Ltd
Unit 5 Riverside, Brambleside
Bellbrook Industrial Estate
Uckfield, East Sussex
TN22 1QQ England

Tel: +44 (0)1825 749494

www.naval-military-press.com
www.nmarchive.com

*In reprinting in facsimile from the original, any imperfections are inevitably reproduced
and the quality may fall short of modern type and cartographic standards.*

PREFACE

CHIEF STAFF-INSTRUCTOR J. O'NEIL, who has held for over six years the position of Boxing Instructor at the Royal Naval School of Physical Training, has compiled this book principally with the object of assisting those who have a knowledge of the art of Boxing, and who wish to teach it to beginners. Although the author has taught and had the training of many excellent boxers, he has of late years devoted his talents mainly to the encouragement of youngsters, particularly to those who, though not born pugilists, and by no means ambitious for high distinction in the Ring, love boxing for its own sake and for the healthy and manly exercise it provides, and wish to improve their knowledge and style, so that they may get the utmost out of the sport, each according to his ability. To these the book should prove of service. A careful study of the illustrations and descriptions will show the soundness of these lessons. They have been evolved after many years of practical boxing, and great experience in training instructors in the art of teaching. Even the expert will find within the pages of this book much to assist him and to improve his style.

B. T. COOTE, *Commander.*

SUPERINTENDENT,
  ROYAL NAVAL SCHOOL OF PHYSICAL
    TRAINING, PORTSMOUTH.

February, 1919.

CONTENTS

Part I
GENERAL REMARKS ON CLASS INSTRUCTION ..   **PAGE** 1

Part II
LESSONS WITH ILLUSTRATIONS 3

Part III
GENERAL NOTES AND ADVICE **59**

Part IV
HINTS ON TRAINING 64

LIST OF PLATES

THE AUTHOR'S FAVOURITE POSE ... ... *Frontispiece*	
	PAGE
"ON GUARD" POSITION	7
LEFT LEAD AT HEAD, AND GUARD FOR SAME	13
LEFT STOP AND RIGHT GUARD FOR LEFT HOOK OR SWING AT JAW	15
LEFT LEAD AT MARK AND GUARD FOR SAME	17
LEFT STOP AND RIGHT CUT FOR LEFT LEAD AT MARK	19
LEFT LEAD TO JAW WITH RIGHT TO FOLLOW TO JAW...	21
LEFT LEAD TO JAW WITH RIGHT TO FOLLOW TO SHORT RIBS	22
LEFT LEAD TO MARK WITH RIGHT TO FOLLOW TO JAW ...	23
SLIPPING A LEFT LEAD AND COUNTERING WITH LEFT TO MARK	24
SLIPPING A LEFT LEAD AND COUNTERING WITH LEFT TO JAW	27
SLIPPING AND COUNTERING WITH RIGHT TO SHORT RIBS...	28
RIGHT HAND CROSS-COUNTER	31
CROSS-COUNTER WITH A SHIFT	32
SIDE-STEPPING TO LEFT AND COUNTERING WITH RIGHT TO JAW	35
DUCKING A LEFT SWING AND SENDING LEFT HOOK TO MARK	36
BLOCKING A LEFT LEAD	39
DEVIATING A LEFT LEAD AT HEAD	40
DEVIATING A LEFT LEAD FOLLOWED BY LEFT HOOK TO MARK	43
BACK MOVING A LEFT LEAD AND COUNTERING WITH RIGHT UPPER-CUT TO JAW	44
PIVOTING TO THE RIGHT AND COUNTERING WITH A LEFT HOOK TO THE JAW	47
LEFT HOOK COUNTER TO JAW WITH RIGHT TO FOLLOW TO STOMACH	48
UPPER-CUTTING UNDER OPPONENT'S LEAD BY A SHIFT OF THE FEET	51
DOUBLE COUNTERS	52
IN-FIGHTING	57
COVERING UP...	58

THE ART OF BOXING
AND HINTS ON TRAINING

Part I

GENERAL REMARKS ON CLASS INSTRUCTION

1. Classes should never be formed up in ranks, but should work in pairs independently.

2. For demonstration of the different positions and movements required, the Instructor should form the class round him, then select one of them and show what is required, after which the class should be paired off and told to practise it.

3. Sharp words of command should be avoided by the Instructor at all times, as they tend to make a drill movement of the required performance, which will result in it becoming stiff and mechanical.

He should talk to the class as if he were talking to an individual pupil.

4. Each pair should work as "master" and "pupil" in turn, and so work each other up in execution and instructing.

5. The Instructor should always have gloves on, correcting and encouraging the class when necessary.

6. The pairs should be changed for each lesson, that they may become familiar with different styles.

7. Any indication of temper should at once be put down by the Instructor. Flash or showy work should not be encouraged.

N.B.—The Instructor should keep the class under control and gain their confidence, be ready to answer questions, and make the instruction as interesting as possible, not insisting on a stereotyped form of explanation.

Part II

LESSONS WITH ILLUSTRATIONS

Lesson 1.—"On Guard" Position—Sparring—Stepping In—Stepping Back.

Lesson 2. — Side Stepping — Distance — Breaking Ground.

Lesson 3.—Left Lead at Head—Guard for Left Lead at Head—Stop for Left Lead at Head.

Lesson 4.—Left Lead at Mark—Guard for Left Lead at Mark—Stop for Left Lead at Mark.

Lesson 5.—Double Leads.

Lesson 6.—Slipping—Slipping to the Right and Countering with the Left Hand.

Lesson 7.—Slipping to the Left and Countering with the Right Hand.

Lesson 8.—Cross-counter.

Lesson 9.—Side-Stepping and Countering.

Lesson 10.—Ducking—Blocking.

Lesson 11.—Deviating—Back Moving.

Lesson 12.—Hook Hits—Upper-cuts.

Lesson 13.—Double Counters.

Lesson 14.—Feinting—Feinting and Drawing.

Lesson 15.—In-fighting.

Loose Play.

LESSON 1.

" ON GUARD."

The body turned partially to the right, the left foot advanced a convenient distance to the left front and flat on the ground, the right heel raised, both knees slightly bent, the body inclined forward from the rear foot. The left hand extended as high as the chin, with the thumb uppermost, elbow well bent and turned down. The right arm lying diagonally across the body, with the hand as high as the breast. The head lowered and the chin inside of the left shoulder. Hands closed without being clenched. The whole position free from restraint and well balanced.

"On Guard" Position.

STEPPING IN.

Move the left foot forward a short distance, and immediately bring the right foot up a similar distance, thus maintaining the original base.

STEPPING BACK.

Move the right foot back a short distance, and immediately bring the left foot back a similar distance, thus maintaining the original base.

Both movements should be stealthy and close to the ground.

In these two movements, as well as in all other footwork movements, the feel of the ground should never be lost.

Common Faults.—Raising and stamping the left foot; moving flat-footed; jumping and moving both feet at once.

SPARRING.

Keep the left hand moving forward and backward and the right hand making a small circle in front of and close to the body, the whole movement being supple and under control.

N.B.—The term "sparring" does not mean the working of the hands only, but in conjunction with foot-work, thus moving about the ring quickly or slowly as occasion demands.

LESSON 2.

SIDE-STEPPING.

Side-step to the left. As for stepping in, except that the left foot is moved to the left front, with the right foot following to its original base.

Side-step to the right. May be done in two ways:—

(1) Move the right foot directly to the right, immediately followed by the left, resuming the original position.

(2) Move the left foot back in line with the right, and immediately carry the right foot to the right, and the left to its original position.

The latter method is a quick way of avoiding a rush or of getting out of a corner, the body ducking to the right at the same time.

DISTANCE

Is the distance between two boxers when sparring, and should be such that before either can hit his opponent he must first step in.

This is a very important factor, as will be proved as the class progresses. Successful judging of distance is only gained by practice. To lead out of distance means that your blow will fall short, and consequently leave you helpless to your opponent's counter. On the other hand, to get too close before starting your attack will endanger you to receiving a stop hit from your opponent.

BREAKING GROUND.

To break ground is to assume the defensive, and may be done either by retiring or by moving to the left or right. This is often done to draw opponent's lead.

LESSON 3.

LEFT LEAD AT HEAD.

Step in as already described in previous lesson, and without changing the position of the hand deliver a straight punch at the jaw, the weight of the body backing up the punch by pressing strongly off the ball of the right foot, the head turned slightly to the right and lowered, the right elbow close to the body with the back of the hand turned towards the jaw. The left hand should be firmly clenched, and the right glove open. After having delivered the blow, step back on guard as quickly as possible, being careful that the hands are not allowed to drop.

N.B.—It is well to mention here that the left lead is the key to attack, and a prominent factor in defence, and should be practised at the commencement of every lesson.

Common Faults.—Not bringing the rear foot up when stepping in; reaching and not letting the body go forward; head not lowered and turned to the right; right hand not kept up.

GUARD FOR LEFT LEAD AT HEAD.

Keeping the right arm across the body, turn the palm of the hand to the front, at the same time turning the head slightly to the right, and bury the chin in the glove, the left hand being kept up.

This guard, if executed as above, will protect the jaw from all blows excepting a left hook.

Common Faults.—Hand held away from jaw; head not turned and lowered; left hand not kept up.

LEFT LEAD AT HEAD, AND GUARD FOR SAME.

LEFT STOP AND RIGHT GUARD FOR LEFT HOOK OR SWING AT JAW.

Without moving the feet, brace up both legs, twist the body from the hips to the right, and allowing the shoulder to go well forward, shoot out the left hand straight to the jaw. At the same time raise the right forearm perpendicularly, and ward off the blow by strongly contracting the arm. Keep the chin well lowered.

LEFT STOP AND RIGHT GUARD FOR LEFT HOOK OR SWING AT JAW.

LESSON 4.

LEFT LEAD AT MARK.

Step in as before, with the body bent well forward from the hips, the head lowered, and deliver a blow at the mark. The elbow to be well bent, with the forearm horizontal, the wrist straight, and the thumb uppermost. The right forearm held perpendicularly and clear of the head, with the knuckles of the hand turned to the front, and as high as the crown of the head, offering a strong resistance against opponent's left.

This lead must be executed with dash and vigour, as it is essential that you should step well in inside opponent's left hand to make the blow effective.

Common Faults.—Not stepping well in; not lowering the head; the right hand not kept up.

GUARD FOR LEFT LEAD AT MARK.

Strongly contract the abdominal muscles and, drawing the stomach well in, force the right arm farther across the body so that the elbow covers the mark, the right hand being kept up, covering the jaw. The left upper arm close in to the side, with the right hand ready to block opponent's right.

Common Faults.—Bringing the hands down to guard, and not using the elbows; not contracting strongly.

LEFT LEAD AT MARK AND GUARD FOR SAME.

STOP FOR LEFT LEAD AT MARK.

Brace up both legs to their fullest extent, draw the stomach in, and at the same time shoot out the left hand straight to opponent's jaw, slightly twisting the body from the hips to allow the shoulder to go well forward, the right hand cutting downwards and outwards in case the stop misses or fails.

LEFT STOP AND RIGHT CUT FOR LEFT LEAD AT MARK.

LESSON 5.

DOUBLE LEADS.

As the term implies, a double lead is one punch immediately following another, and should always be done with the left leading. Step in and deliver a left lead at either head or mark, and on the same advance follow up with a smashing right-hand punch at either head or short ribs.

Three good examples :—

    Left and right at head.
    Left at head and right at short ribs.
    Left at mark and right at head.

The success of this attack depends entirely upon the rapidity with which the second blow follows the first. To gain this rapidity it is essential that the left blow should be a fairly light one. Immediately withdrawing it and swinging the body to the left, throw all the weight of the body into the second punch, this being the desired blow.

The left hand, when withdrawn, should be kept up, ready to block opponent's right.

This attack is generally successful and effective against a nervous opponent, one who will seldom or never lead.

Common Faults.—Stiffening the arm in the first lead, thereby propping opponent off and stopping your advance for the second punch; reaching with the right hand instead of twisting the body and allowing the rear foot to come up; not lowering the head.

LEFT LEAD TO JAW WITH RIGHT TO FOLLOW TO JAW.

Left Lead to Jaw with Right to follow to Short Ribs.

LEFT LEAD TO MARK WITH RIGHT TO FOLLOW TO JAW.

SLIPPING A LEFT LEAD AND COUNTERING WITH LEFT TO MARK.

LESSON 6.

SLIPPING

Is a method used to avoid opponent's lead at head, and can be done either to the right or left.

SLIPPING TO THE RIGHT.

Twist the head and body quickly to the right, at the same time bending slightly forward, and cause the blow to pass over the left shoulder.

SLIPPING TO THE LEFT.

The same as for slipping to the right, excepting that the movement is made the reverse way.

It is important here that the left hand should be kept up and the head down, as the movement is made towards opponent's right hand; the left hand should be ready to block its use.

SLIPPING TO THE RIGHT AND COUNTERING WITH THE LEFT AT MARK.

Slip as described; at the same time holding the forearm horizontal with the elbow close to the side, deliver a blow at the mark, pressing from the ball of the right foot to back up the punch.

SLIPPING TO THE RIGHT AND COUNTERING WITH THE LEFT AT JAW.

Slip as before, but, bracing up both legs, deliver an upward punch under the jaw.

SLIPPING A LEFT LEAD AND COUNTERING WITH LEFT TO JAW.

SLIPPING AND COUNTERING WITH RIGHT TO SHORT RIBS.

LESSON 7.

SLIPPING TO THE LEFT AND COUNTERING WITH THE RIGHT HAND AT SHORT RIBS.

Slip as before described, and, keeping the forearm horizontal with the elbow close to the side, at the same time pressing from the rear foot, deliver a blow at the short ribs.

N.B.—This is a very effective counter, but the points mentioned in Lesson 6 should be strictly observed.

Common Faults.—Not combining the two movements, viz., slipping and countering; not getting the push from the rear foot.

LESSON 8.

CROSS-COUNTERS. SLIPPING TO THE LEFT AND CROSS-COUNTERING WITH THE RIGHT HAND.

Slip opponent's lead as before, and at the same time bracing up from the rear foot, raise the elbow outwards, and deliver a corkscrew punch at the jaw, the hand travelling over and as close to opponent's arm as possible straight from the shoulder. The left hand should be kept up as before.

RIGHT HAND CROSS-COUNTER.

CROSS-COUNTER WITH A SHIFT.

CROSS-COUNTER WITH A SHIFT.

With a quick shift of the right foot forward outside opponent's left, and the left foot swinging to the rear, deliver a downward punch at the jaw as in previous cross-counter.

Common Faults.—Not combining the movement; swinging; keeping the left foot fast.

LESSON 9.

SIDE-STEPPING AND COUNTERING AT MARK.

Side-step to the left as described in Lesson 2, thus causing the blow to pass wide; at the same time bracing up both legs, and with the forearm horizontal, twist the body to the left and deliver a blow at the mark. The left hand should be kept up ready to act.

SIDE-STEPPING AND COUNTERING AT JAW.

Side-step to the left as before, and bracing up the legs as before, keeping the upper arm close to the side, deliver a blow upwards under the jaw. Left hand as before.

This latter method, if correctly executed, is a damaging counter to an opponent who keeps his head low when leading, and you find that you cannot get to his jaw with a cross-counter.

Common Faults.—Stepping too wide and not moving forward; not bracing the legs and twisting the body.

SIDE-STEPPING TO LEFT AND COUNTERING WITH RIGHT TO JAW.

DUCKING A LEFT SWING AND SENDING LEFT HOOK TO MARK

LESSON 10.

DUCKING

Is a method generally used to avoid hooks or swings at the head, but should not be used to avoid straight blows. To duck, further bend both knees, lower the head, and at the same time step to the right with right foot, causing the intended blow to pass over the head.

This movement is generally made to the right, and is the best way of getting out of a corner.

BLOCKING.

To block an opponent is to prevent him carrying out his intention, and may be done as follows :—

(1) To block a left lead. If an opponent makes some preliminary movement, such as drawing the arm back preparatory to leading, or shuffling the feet, act at once, straighten up to full height, and turning the body to the right, place your left hand against your opponent's biceps or shoulder, and so prevent him from leading.

(2) After slipping opponent's lead to the left, and countering with the right hand (the movement being made towards opponent's right hand, to prevent the use of that hand), place your own left hand upon his forearm or glove.

Care should be taken not to hold.

BLOCKING A LEFT LEAD.

DEVIATING A LEFT LEAD AT HEAD.

LESSON 11.

DEVIATING.

To deviate a left lead at head, strike opponent's hand, wrist, or forearm a sharp beat with the palm of the right hand, deviating it from the line of attack. This invariably puts him off his balance, and renders him helpless.

The beat should be made from the elbow and not from the shoulder, and should be sharp and decisive without following the action. The left hand should be dropped so as not to arrest opponent's upset.

Common Faults.—Acting too late; pushing and following the movement.

DEVIATING A LEFT LEAD FOLLOWED BY LEFT HOOK TO MARK.

BACK MOVING A LEFT LEAD AND COUNTERING WITH RIGHT UPPER-CUT TO JAW.

BACK MOVING.

To back move a lead, step back a very short pace with the right foot, and at the same time sway the body slightly backwards, transferring the weight of the body to the rear foot, thus causing the intended blow to fall shot.

This movement should be practised in conjunction with deviating. If accurately timed and well under control, both hands should be free for countering. An upper-cut with either hand, or a short right to the side of the head, would not be amiss. To deviate a left lead without "back moving" turns an opponent on to a "left hook" either at head or mark, preferably the latter.

Common Faults.—Stepping back too far; swaying too far and losing balance.

LESSON 12.

HOOK HITS

Should not be encouraged as a method of attack, as they invariably develop into swinging, and will surely fail against a straight stop from the left hand. As a counter blow, after having beaten opponent's lead, they are very damaging, and most awkward blows to guard against.

LEFT HOOK COUNTERS TO JAW.

By bracing up both legs and pivoting on the ball of both feet, twist the body to the right; at the same time raising the elbow and turning the back of the hand up, deliver a blow at the jaw. The right hand is to be kept up.

Pivoting to the Right and Countering with a Left Hook to the Jaw.

LEFT HOOK COUNTER TO JAW WITH RIGHT TO FOLLOW TO STOMACH.

LEFT HOOK COUNTER TO MARK.

Slip opponent's lead to the right as before described, and, keeping the knees bent, press forward from the rear foot and deliver a blow at the mark, raising the elbow as before. The head should be lowered well inside the left shoulder.

Common Faults.—Drawing the arm back; not raising the elbow and getting the twist of the body; making too wide a movement.

N.B.—Right hook counter has already been described in Lesson 9, viz., side-stepping to the left and countering to jaw.

UPPER-CUTS

Are generally used against an opponent who crouches, or reaches when leading, instead of stepping in, or against a lead that has been made to fall short by back moving. To deliver the blow, turn the knuckles up, and keeping the upper arm close to the body, brace up both legs and direct the blow under the jaw.

N.B.—To upper-cut with the left hand is not a favourite movement, and has little to recommend it, owing to the position of the hand when sparring.

Upper-cutting under Opponent's Lead by a Shift of the Feet.

DOUBLE COUNTERS.

LESSON 13.

DOUBLE COUNTERS.

The term double counter should not be taken literally as in the case of a double lead (the latter being a premeditated double attack), but depends wholly upon circumstances, and is not a premeditated action. After having countered with one hand, presumably with good effect, any opening for a second counter with the other hand should at once be taken advantage of, hence the second hand should be kept ready.

Example.—Side-stepping to the left and countering to the mark with the right hand, followed by a left hook to the jaw.

The opening for the second counter may accrue from two reasons :—

(1) The first counter, having a hurtful effect, would probably bring opponent's head forward and his guard down.
(2) Dropping his right hand when leading, thus leaving the jaw exposed.

LESSON 14.

FEINTS.

A feint is any movement made with the intention of deceiving your opponent, and should be made as realistic as possible, the object being to make opponent guard that part of the target feinted at, and so make the opening required for the real attack.

Examples:—
1. Feint at head and lead at mark.
2. Feint at mark and lead at head.

To make the feint realistic and effective, make a forward movement of the whole body from the feet up, expression playing an important part, and the movement well under control. This may be repeated two or three times, and against a nervous opponent will have him nonplussed and easy to attack.

FEINTING AND DRAWING.

To draw an opponent is to induce him to perform the lead or counter required. Drawing a lead is usually done by breaking ground and intentionally leaving an opening.

To draw a particular or favourite counter, lead once or twice warily to encourage the counter in mind, then make a feint lead, and drawing the desired counter, guard it, and counter in return.

Example.—A cross-counter being a favourite with most boxers, encourage it by one or two light leads. The next time feint lead, and taking the counter on the left forearm, at the same time stepping up with the right foot, deliver a right hook inside to the jaw.

Common Fault.—Delay in following up the intended action after the draw.

LESSON 15.

IN-FIGHTING

Is a valuable asset to a short and stocky man, but should not be overdone.

To get in for in-fighting, first slip or parry opponent's lead, then with the head lowered and the body bent well forward from the hip, pressing away from the rear foot, deliver a series of short arm blows at the body. This will invariably bring down opponent's guard, when an occasional left hook to the jaw could be tried.

N.B.—To make the punching at the body effective, keep the elbows close to the side, twisting the body with each blow, pressing forward all the time.

LOOSE PLAY.

Practise the different methods of attack and defence already taught, paying special attention to "judging of distance," "footwork," "timing," etc., and hitting correctly. Short bouts between Instructor and the class (each in turn) might now be indulged in, as a means of encouraging the class to act on their own initiative.

IN-FIGHTING.

COVERING UP.

Part III

GENERAL NOTES AND ADVICE

POISE OF THE BODY.

It is most essential that the body should be free from restraint whilst sparring, so that you will be ready at any moment to brace up everything and throw the whole weight into a blow. By keeping all muscles relaxed until the time for action, you are able to move about with agility, which would not be the case if the body were held at high tension all the time, besides having a tiring effect on the whole system.

FOOTWORK.

A boxer moving about the ring should do so in a stealthy manner, the right heel being always clear of the ground, and the foremost foot ever on the slide. The feel of the ground should never be lost. Nothing looks more cumbersome than a flat-footed boxer.

Too little attention is paid to footwork. To stand and exchange punch for punch is not boxing, and may be all right with two men of the same calibre, but pitted against a clever, shifty boxer, a man who relies on his big punch, and has no idea of footwork, will be all at sea, wasting his punches in the air and, above all, wasting his strength, and in the end beating himself. A boxer who can use his feet as well as his hands very seldom gets punished to any extent; he will minimize the power of a punch by back moving or side-stepping with scarcely an effort, thus having both hands for punching.

SPARRING.

The hands should never be allowed to drop below the waist line. During a long period of sparring, and when well out of distance, a rest can be obtained by laying the hands across the body, being then ever ready for instant attack or defence. At close quarters, always try to keep your hands above your opponent's.

ATTACK.

In all straight hits, which should be delivered from the shoulder, the back of the hands should be outwards, with the thumb uppermost, and tightly clenched with the wrist straight. This will prevent injury to the thumb or wrist and insure the blow being struck with the knuckles. It is a good practice when leading or countering with the left hand to turn the head partially to the right, and *vice versa;* by so doing you will possibly miss altogether opponent's probable return, or at least save your mouth and nose from being hit.

Avoid drawing the arm back before hitting, thereby making known your intention (which is commonly termed " telegraphing "). Vary your methods according to the style and strength of your opponent; in plain words, use your brains.

For example, if your opponent be much taller, and possesses a good left hand, it is useless to box him at out-distance; your plan should be to force him and get to close quarters, put him off his game, and give him no chance to out-box you. This is easier said than done, but with a man who is as good a boxer, or better than yourself, it is your only chance. On the other hand, it should be his game to use his advantage of reach, combined always with footwork, to keep you out and box at long range. Should your opponent lead with hooks, or swings, work on the defensive; let him start the attack, and with a good straight left, accurately timed, and a sound guard, you will invariably stop him. Have no half-measures about your work.

DEFENCE.

When on the defensive keep your opponent just out of striking distance; when he advances, you retire, and *vice versa*. Always be on the alert for his attack, but should your opponent delay his attack and get within distance, reverse the positions by at once shooting out your left hand, and return to the defensive again. That would be bad judgment of distance on his part.

COMPETITION.

In competitions many a good boxer loses a bout by depending too much on his punch to gain the award. As a competition is only limited to bouts of three rounds, with an occasional fourth round (extra round), a good boxer will often find himself a loser by being too anxious to procure a knock-out, his opponent meanwhile doing all the attacking, and thus collecting the points and invariably gaining the referee's decision. In short bouts of this description a boxer should always try to obtain the balance of points, at the same time being ever ready to seize an opportunity for a knockout. The last round especially should be devoted to attack, but this does not imply that a good defence should not also be maintained. Should an extra round be ordered, through the judges disagreeing, do your utmost to beat your opponent for lead, persevering to the gong. It is worth taking a chance, as the award will surely go to the aggressor.

CONTESTS.

In contests of long duration, viz., six rounds or more, one has longer time in which to study the style and qualities of one's opponent, and can afford to nurse oneself until one has gauged his strength and methods.

Part IV

HINTS ON TRAINING

It is a great mistake to lay down a definite routine of daily work to be carried out. By so doing, apart from its not being suitable for all men, training becomes mechanical, and very soon wearisome, which should be most strictly avoided.

Training should be made a pleasure and not a hardship. As soon as a man commences to feel fatigued, he should cease work for the day.

A man cannot be made to train; he can be made to go through a certain amount of work after a fashion, but unless he performs it willingly and conscientiously, it might as well be left undone.

WORK REQUIRED OF A BOXER TO GET FIT.

Plenty of walking, at a good swinging pace, in the open country, where he can inhale pure, fresh air, and so improve his breathing, is most essential.

If he wants to reduce weight, he should dress accordingly. A short sprint of about 50 yards at top speed occasionally during the walk is beneficial for the wind and quick action.

The distance covered should depend upon the feelings of the person concerned.

On returning, a douche in warm water, followed by cold, and then a brisk rubbing with towels.

GYMNASIUM WORK

Should consist of suitable Swedish exercises, particularly Abdominal and Lateral; Skipping, Medicine Bag, Shadow Boxing, Punch Ball and Bag, and Boxing.

SWEDISH EXERCISES.

A light Swedish table, including strong abdominal and lateral exercises.

Abdominal.—Lying on the back at full stretch, the hands above the head, grasping some fixed apparatus, raise the legs alternately to an angle of 75 degrees, the leg that is lowered being kept just clear of the ground. After repeating this exercise about half a dozen times, raise both legs straight together, increasing the number of times as you feel like it. Follow this exercise by quickly bringing the knees up to the chest, thus rounding the whole body up; repeat this a few times. Another practice, after rounding up, is to keep in that position and work the legs as in bicycle movement, increasing and decreasing speed. Boat-pulling, being a strong abdominal exercise, can be substituted by fixing the feet and going through the motions of rowing.

It is not intended that the exercises mentioned above should be gone through daily, or in the prescribed order. They are an assortment of exercises recommended for developing the abdominal muscles.

Lateral.—Any form of turnings, twistings, and bendings, standing, kneeling, or lying, or even when moving about, will produce the suppleness of body required.

SKIPPING

Should not consist of simply marking time in one particular spot, but should be of a varied nature, viz., moving backward and forward, turning and twisting, side-stepping, etc. It should not be indulged in to excess. As skipping means being on the toes, it has a very hardening effect on the calves, and tends to make one muscle-bound, which invariably produces leg weariness.

MEDICINE BAG.

A bag of split peas or beans, placed inside an old football case, the whole weighing from 3 to 5 lbs. In company with one or more sparring partners, assume a boxing attitude, and, keeping on the move, put the bag from one to the other, rapidly increasing and decreasing the distance, decreasing for speed and increasing for power. The "put" should be delivered in the same manner as a straight punch is delivered, viz., from the shoulder, and not as in throwing. It should be received by catching, guarding, twisting, turning. A sparring attitude should be maintained until time is called.

SHADOW BOXING.

Boxing an imaginary opponent by going through all manner of blows, guarding, side-stepping, covering up, and working up speed in footwork.

It is beneficial, when possible, to do this before a full-sized mirror, thus having your own reflection to size up.

PUNCH BALL

Is useful for punching practice and footwork, but is apt to become monotonous.

PUNCHING BAG.

Should be weighted from 28 to 56 lbs.; a canvas bag about 18 inches long by 3 feet in circumference, stuffed with oakum to the required weight, a small wire passing through the centre with a toggle at the lower end, and an eye at the top end. As the bag is filled and pounded down, the toggle will draw close up, and so counter-sink the bottom of the bag, which is as it should be, protecting the knuckles from injury when practising uppercuts.

This is an invaluable article to a boxer in training; it develops the forearm, wrist, and hands, and invariably the punch; it can be hung anywhere; it makes no noise, and is fast or slow, according to the mood of the man.

BOXING.

Real boxing should be indulged in as much as possible, and with as many different opponents as possible, as each one is sure to present a difference in style or action.

When I say real boxing, I mean "to go all out." It is a great mistake to indulge in tapping and fancy work, and holding punches back will do more harm than good. Get good men to box with you, men who are not averse to having a mix up, or receiving and giving a punch. If a blow is to be delivered correctly, it must necessarily be delivered with "snap," and "snap" means speed. Get real boxing, and plenty of it, when training, and it will invariably assert itself when needed; at the same time it brings out all the methods of defence when boxing in real earnest.

It is a mistake to continue boxing right up to the actual day of combat, especially when going through a long course of training, as apart from risking injury to hands, etc., the eagerness which one should have when one steps into the ring is lost. To retain that eagerness it is advisable to discard the gloves at least a week before the actual day, and so avoid any signs of staleness. A good feeling that one should have when going into the ring for a serious encounter is a firm grip of the hands and an eagerness to get started. If the grip is lacking, that is surely a sign of staleness.

MASSAGE.

A thorough kneading from head to foot after a hot and cold shower will finish the work for the day. Guard against catching cold, and forget the work until to-morrow.

The old system of pounding and punching the muscles as a form of massage was not only erroneous, but did more harm than good; instead of removing stiffness and having an exhilarating effect on the whole body, it left the principal sore and tied up in knots, so to speak, and consequently he dreaded what was in store for him, whereas proper massage has the reverse effect.

DIET.

"One man's meat is another man's poison," so decide for yourself.

A Selection Of Classic Instructive Titles Relating To The Art Of Pugilism & Self Defence In Both War & Peace
Find our entire selection @ naval-military-press.com

ALL-IN FIGHTING
The distilled knowledge of W.E. Fairbairn, legendary SOE instructor in unarmed combat, and inventor of the Sykes-Fairbairn knife, who learned his deadly skills in 30 years on the Shanghai waterfront. Fully illustrated.
9781847348531

ART OF BOXING AND SCIENCE OF SELF DEFENCE
Former Lightweight Champion Billy Edwards shares the techniques and strategies of the sweet science in his beautifully illustrated boxing guide. Explore boxing's transition from bare knuckle spectacle to today's Marquis of Queensbury ruleset.
9781474539548

SELF DEFENCE OR THE ART OF BOXING

Ned Donnelly was a pioneer of boxing training during the late Victorian era. Explore the strategies and techniques used by this trainer of champions via a series of easy-to-follow illustrations and clear, concise coaching steps.

9781474539562

JACK GOODWIN'S BOXING

This 1920's boxing masterpiece by Jack Goodwin puts you in the shoes of a coach in that era. Uncover the best ways to run, manage and train boxers as taught by Jack Goodwin, a champion and trainer of champions in the noble science.

9781474539586

THE COMPLETE BOXER

Gunner Moir provides detailed instructions on the techniques he deployed to become British Heavyweight Champion. Taught in a series of easy to learn techniques, combinations, and boxing strategies.

9781474539609

ART OF WRESTLING

George de Relwyskow Army Gymnastic Staff

In the appreciation to this book Captain Daniels, V.C., M.C., Rifle Brigade, states: "In adding a word to this book on the style of wrestling as taught at the Headquarters Gymnasium of the British Army, and having had personal experience in the various holds and throws taught, I consider it has been of great value in the training of the soldier, and the bringing out of those qualities of grit and determination which have been seen in all ranks who have taken an active part throughout the greatest war in history." 1919.

9781783313563

KILL OR GET KILLED

Rex Applegate's "kill or be killed" helped prepare America's marines, soldiers, sailors, spies and airmen for the realities of war. This highly shared and respected work provides all you need to know about unarmed combat and close quarter engagement with the enemy.

9781474539661

BOXING (V-Five)
The Aviation Training Office of the Chief of Naval Operations
The game-changing V-Five suite of training manuals helped get a generation of American aviators fit for war. Here we explore how the airmen of the US navy trained in boxing as part of their military fitness regime.
9781474539623

THE TEXTBOOK OF WRESTLING
Get your wrestling skills matt-ready from wrestling champion and world-renown trainer Ernest Gruhn. Replete with detailed holds, throws, pins and strategies for success in a wide range of wrestling rulesets.
9781474539647

MANUAL OF PHYSICAL TRAINING 1914
(United States Army)
Published just prior to the outbreak of World War 1, this beautifully illustrated guide was designed to revolutionise the combat fitness and readiness of the US Army covering a wide range of gymnastic and combat calisthenic exercises.
9781474539708

DEAL THE FIRST DEADLY BLOW
United States Department of the Army
This Vietnam-era classic showcases in detail how the US Forces trained in close quarter combat. Known as the "encyclopaedia of combat" it helped a generation learn how to become devastating effective with empty hands, knives and bayonets alike.
9781474539722

HAND-TO-HAND COMBAT
Bureau of Aeronautics U.S Navy 1943

This is one of the best combative manuals from World War 2, developed by the US Navy V-Five Staff, that included the renowned American wrestler Wesley Brown. It is then not especially surprising that wrestling skills predominate in this manual, and form the base skill-set for this combative system.

9781474537391

ABWEHR ENGLISCHER GANGSTER METHODEN DEFENSE OF ENGLISH GANGSTERS METHODS – SILENT KILLING – FULL ENGLISH TRANSLATION

In 1942 the Wehrmacht published a training manual with the goal of countering the "silent killing" tactics used by the British commando units. The manual was – much in line with typical National Socialist terminology –titled
"Abwehr Englischer Gangster-methoden" or "Defence Against English Gangster methods".

This book was compiled due the Wehrmacht intelligence operatives uncovering of a British hand-to-hand course for the SOE, Commandos, et al, on methods of quick and silent killing (undoubtedly developed by W. E. Fairbairn and E. A. Sykes). They correctly assessed that their troops in general and particularly the Geheime Staatspolizei (Gestapo), Sicherheitsdienst (SD), their security guards, and sentries would be in grave danger when confronted by men trained in these methods. This manual/program was the Wehrmacht's response.

9781474538336

BOXING FOR BOYS

Regtl. Sergt.-Major & B Dent Army Gymnastic Headquarters

A successful system of boxing instruction for large classes, to allow tuition with no detriment to the "backward or shy pupil". Covers Kit-On, Guard-Sparring-Advance-Point & Mark-Ducking-Medicine, Bag-Left & Right Hooks etc. The author considered that boxing systematically taught to the youth was beneficial exercise, and would have a marked elevating influence on the national character.

9781783314607

HAND-TO-HAND FIGHTING

A System Of Personal Defence For The Soldier (1918)

A tough book on the art of hand to hand fighting in the trenches of the Great War. Demonstrating techniques utilised to "do away with the enemy", many of which are barred in clean wrestling, the book includes good clear photographic illustrations presenting important attack methods including the "Hammer Lock", "Kidney Kick", "Head Twist", "Knee Groin Kick", and the "Knee Break", all very important in a man to man, life or death encounter, when fighting in the mud of the trenches.

9781783313983

HAND TO HAND COMBAT

Francois d'Eliscu taught thousands of U.S. Army Rangers how to fight down and dirty in World War II. d'Eliscu doesn't get the press that Fairbairn and Applegate do, but he did a commendable job writing this book. It is basic, meant for training raw recruits in a short amount of time before sending them to the front, but simple is good when you are in combat, as most combative experts' will tell you.

9781474535823

COLD STEEL

A cold-war combatives classic. John Styers, US Marine and WW2 veteran, lays out his approach to close quarters combat with rifle, bayonet, stick, knife and empty hands. Explore what helped wartime and post-war Marines stay ahead of the competition with lucid imagery and clear combative descriptions.

9781474540643

THE COMPLETE KANO JIU-JITSU

Join world-famous physical culture expert H. Irving Hancock, and Jiu-Jitsu specialist Katsukama Higashi as they showcase the art of 'Kano Jiu-Jitsu' now known as Judo. Get an exclusive glimpse into the transitional era of the martial art, alongside how it uses Japanese physical culture methodologies for self-improvement.

9781474540735

WE Fairbairn's Complete Compendium of Lethal, Unarmed, Hand-to-Hand Combat Methods and Fighting In Colour

All 844 images of Fairbairn and his assistants can now for the first time be seen in full colour, lending a clarity to the practical methods of mastering the manner of dealing with an assailant, both in time of war and when placed in difficulty during unpleasant modern urban situations. These various holds, trips, kicks, blows etc, allow the average man or woman a position of security against almost any form of armed or unarmed attack. Captain W.E. Fairbairn would have approved of this new colour version, that gives an illustrative clarity to the original that was lacking in previous monochrome reprints of his work.

All six of W.E. Fairbairn's works in one binding to create the ultimate colour compendium: Get Tough-All-In Fighting-Shooting to Live-Scientific Self-Defence-Hands Off!-Defend

9781783318735

SELF DEFENCE FOR WOMEN COMBATO

Join the Canadian combatives legend William "Bill" Underwood as he showcases self-defence for women. Over the course of clear photography, sketches and instructions he lays out a curriculum for self-defence for the attacks women would be most likely to face.

9781474540711

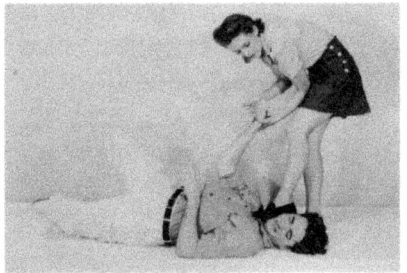

SCIENTIFIC UNARMED COMBAT
The Art of Dynamic Self-Defence

Learn the esoteric Sri Lankan art of 'Cheena-Adi' with R. A Vairamuttu. This guide explores armed and unarmed self-defence drawing heavily from Indian martial culture, alongside wellness and development from Indian physical culture, fitness, diet and medicine.

9781474540728

THE NEW SCIENCE
Weaponless Defence

Join wrestling champions Prof F. S Lewis, William V Gregory and Boxing Champ Tommy Burns as they showcase street orientated self-defence from people with a proven track record of fighting success. This 1906 manual via a series of photos and instructions lays out simple, tried and tested ways to keep yourself safe.

9781474540704

COMBAT CONDITIONING MANUAL
Jiu-Jitsu Defence, Bayonet Defence and Club Defence

This 1942 guide for marines lays out the basics of combat Ju Jitsu as part of an overall training regimen for US Marines. It's a holistic guide that covers defences against armed and unarmed attackers, physical fitness and even first aid.

9781474540698

BOXING TAUGHT THROUGH "SLOW MOTION FILM"

Learn the ropes from the best fighters of the 1900s-1930s in this unique boxing manual. Using stills from super slow-mo fight footage, this treasure trove unpacks the skills, tips and tactics of the champs for you to emulate at home.

9781474540681

HOW TO BOX CORRECTLY

Explore the art of boxing according to famous Bronx boxing brand Ben Lee in this 1944 how-to guide. Learn the ropes from one of the nation's top trainers and boxing journalists John J. Romano, in this warmly illustrated guide to the sweet science.

9781474540674

THE ART OF IN-FIGHTING BY FRANK KLAUS

German-American Middleweight Champ Frank Klaus showcases his KO-scoring boxing IQ in this 1913 guide. Containing clear and easy to understand photography and descriptions, Klaus gives us an insight into the emerging hard-hitting American style of professional boxing.

9781474541473

THE ART OF BOXING AND HINTS ON TRAINING

Crafted just after WW1 in 1919, this guide by Royal Naval Physical Training, Chief Staff Instructor J.O'Neil explores the military benefits of boxing. Showcasing via lucid text and full page photography.

9781474541510

JIM DRISCOLL'S TEXTBOOK OF BOXING

Driscoll was a former Featherweight World Champion and in this 1914 guide, he uses cutting edge and clear photography to showcase the new scientific boxing method. Driscoll showcases to the audience the way to best combine British and American boxing training and fighting philosophy.

9781474541466

JUDO AND ITS USE IN HAND TO HAND COMBAT FROM SEABEES NAVAL ENGINEERING CORPS

Brought to you by William Caldwell of the Seabees Naval Engineering Corps. This WW2 close combat classic provides an insight into the "Combat Judo" used by the navy to prepare personnel for the dangers of theatre. Fully photographed and accessible with clear instructional content to follow.

9781474541480

HAND TO HAND COMBAT – Field Manual 21-150

An example of Cold War / Korean War close combat training. Filled with instructor notes and clear imagery covering unarmed and "cold weapon" combat such as bayonet, knife and garrotte.

9781474541459

AMERICAN JUDO ILLUSTRATED

Brought to you by William Caldwell of the Seabees Naval Engineering Corps. This WW2 close combat classic provides an insight into the "Combat Judo" used by the navy to prepare personnel for the dangers of theatre. Fully photographed and accessible with clear instructional content to follow.

9781474541527

BOXING

This 1906 guide from former English Heavyweight Champion Captain Johnstone, showcases the leading techniques, skills, strategies and fighting philosophies of the day. Brought to life with vivid storytelling from military boxing advocates alongside lucid photography and crisp follow-along guidance for boxers to follow.

9781474541534

KILL OR GET KILLED

Lt Col. Rex Applegate's WW2 Combat Classic 'Kill or Get Killed' is one of the most detailed and comprehensive guides of armed and unarmed combat ever written. From unarmed, to knife, bayonet, pistol, garotte and more – Applegate provides written descriptions, photographs, illustrations on more to showcase and share the skills of forces like the O.S.S.

9781474541541

BALL PUNCHING - A PICTORIAL GUIDE TO THE SPEEDBAG
This 1922 guide from Tom Carpenter is a response to the 'speedbag' craze of the early part of the century. It showcases via clear instructions and photography how to best use tools such as maize, speed and double-end bags for fitness and fighting skills.
9781474541503

SCIENTIFIC BOXING FROM A FISTIC EXPERT
Diet - Fight Training - K.O. Punching
This 1937 guide to the American school and style of professional boxing provides a clear and well-illustrated suite of technical skills and drills to compete successfully. Replete with training advice, rule guidance and ring Generalship principles to help boxers be inline with the latest advice and training acumen.
9781474541497

www.ingramcontent.com/pod-product-compliance
Lightning Source LLC
LaVergne TN
LVHW010318070426
835510LV00031B/3450